DISENCHANTED

A young man's story of Vietnam and his journey home

by

Lane James

The contents of this work, including, but not limited to, the accuracy of events, people, and places depicted; opinions expressed; permission to use previously published materials included; and any advice given or actions advocated are solely the responsibility of the author, who assumes all liability for said work and indemnifies the publisher against any claims stemming from publication of the work.

All Rights Reserved
Copyright © 2019 by Lane James

No part of this book may be reproduced or transmitted, downloaded, distributed, reverse engineered, or stored in or introduced into any information storage and retrieval system, in any form or by any means, including photocopying and recording, whether electronic or mechanical, now known or hereinafter invented without permission in writing from the publisher.

Dorrance Publishing Co
585 Alpha Drive
Pittsburgh, PA 15238
Visit our website at *www.dorrancebookstore.com*

ISBN: 978-1-4809-9498-0
eISBN: 978-1-4809-9571-0

This book is dedicated to my son Matthew Howard James. Such a wonderful man, he was taken from us early in a motorcycle accident. We still have the sign at the store that says, "The Store That Matt Built," as the new renovation was truly his idea, and I still ask him how to do things that need to be done.

Chapter 1

It was hard to realize that I was actually in the army and on my way to Vietnam. At nineteen years of age, it just seemed as if I may as well be flying to Mars. I was sitting in the Flying Tiger airplane seat in severe turbulence heading to Biên Hòa airport in Vietnam, after being drafted to do a two-year stint in the army for something I had no idea about. With half the country against the war and politicians waffling, it just didn't feel like we were going to fight against some great evil like in World War II.

And that's when all hell broke loose! We had that feeling that the plane was dropping out of the sky, and we were all going to die. It was as if the whole plane was in free fall, and people were hitting the ceiling as the plane took a five-hundred-foot drop. Then there was a loud crash as the plane hit bottom and all of us came crashing down with servicemen strewn all over. Seatbelts? Who needs seatbelts! As I crashed into the seat nearest the wings I saw them bend to the point of almost breaking. All the female flight attendants were handing out farewell candy at the time. Seeing some of these ladies (Yes, all flight attendance were ladies back then) injured with candy all over the place got me wondering. If I survived this, was this going to be the last time I was going to see the beauty of an American girl. The sense, smell, and charm that left me with the Stone's song, " You just don't know what ya got until it's gone."

To think that these flight attendants did this on a regular basis, seeing young boys going to this war, knowing full well that most will come back with some mental or physical damage, and then did the return flight carrying home so many injured. They should have received the kind heart award.

Most of our injuries were due to what's called "clear air turbulence." It's invisible to radar, as it's just fast-moving currents of air. Being inside one isn't so bad. It's being above or below one, where the fast-moving air breaks up the slow air all around it. One airline dropped 990 feet but still landed safely. This turbulence is still the number one cause of non-fatal injuries on flights. Most planes today are not only built better but have the technology to avoid some of the serious turbulent areas.

As a funny twist of fate, when I got drafted I was working at Boeing plant two in Seattle as a stretch press operator, and one of our tasks was to stretch the beams that hold the wings together for the 737 and 747 Models. Thank God this was a Douglas aircraft!

As the flight corrected itself, the thought of not getting to Vietnam was ever present. As it turned out, some were injured but most were well, and we eventually landed at the Biên Hòa airport near Saigon

It was Feb 25th, 1969, and the Tet offensive was in full force. The North Vietnamese forces in February, 1969 in South Vietnam during the Vietnam War, one year after the original Tet Offensive.

They would call us greenies, new meat, rookies and many other endearing names that left us feeling like those dreams that you have when you are at school and look down and see you only have your underpants on! So very exposed.

From the plane we were bused to the distribution center, where there was a mix of green new arrivals—with their new bright green colored uniforms, deer in the headlights look, and confused to the max—who had no gun and no idea of what was coming, and the short-timers, who had done their time and were heading home.

Sitting on my duffel bag and asking my friend Mike what he thought was next, we heard our first whistle of rockets being shot at us. It's a sound you never forget. When you hear those damned things, you are always trying to tuck your head inside your shoulders.

All of us ran to dive into the bunker nearby until the shelling was over. I always wondered, who was the idiot who built these two-story barracks just like we had stateside and then put four feet high sandbags around it and thought that was enough protection? Sure as hell not for the guys on the second floor!

As the rockets whistled by, with us curled up as low as possible in that "Momma, come save me" position, one whistled so close and exploded just in front of the bunker. That is when you really appreciate the guys who made that bunker and those sandbags!

And once we thought it was safe to come out and mostly watch how others reacted, we crawled out of the bunker and then heard that sound of rockets again. Diving back into the bunkers for the second time, we also heard a group laughing their asses off and realized they had just pulled the oldest trick in the book to new arrivals. They had whistled the sound of rockets. Bastards! Good Morning Vietnam!

Chapter 2

My home life had always been a cross between a car wreck and a Sunday drive. At nine years-old, life had changed for me. Even though Dad was beating Mom, it was still our family, but when mom got the divorce and we had armed guards around the house because of Dad's threat to kill her, that was the beginning of change for me.

There is a sense of dirty, deep down, that you just can't wash off. It left me feeling incomplete and lost. At that time, divorce was a dirty word.

We were very poor. A portion of the money my brother Bill and I earned from delivering the Seattle PI newspapers went to Mom. There were five of us: Gae, who was one at the time, John at three years old, me, and Bill at eleven. Yes, Dad rarely gave much child support to help keep us keep going. It was up to Mom with a little help from us.

I was an industrious little tyke and turned to the love of animals as my friends to help me through this journey. Mom allowed me to have pigeons on the roof and a duck named Gertrude. At the age of ten I raised Gertrude from a baby and built her a concrete swimming pool and a pen. When I delivered papers, our dog Penny and Gertrude would walk alongside. I think Gertrude thought she was a dog as she quacked her way along the route. The neighbors would come out while I was delivering papers at 6 A.M. just to watch the three of us. On the weekends when we finished, we would go down under the train trestle and go saltwater fishing. Gertrude would go out for a swim and play with some of the other ducks until I called her to come home. One of those great childhood memories. Just unforgettable!

Mom went on to not only learn the guitar but become one of the best classical guitar instructors in the country. She was the head of Seattle's Classical Guitar Society, which put on local concerts, and she would travel once a year to meet with the legendary virtuoso Spanish classical guitarist, Andre Segovia.

Mom received her Bachelor of Arts degree at age fifty and went to become Professor of Music at Seattle Pacific University. As she walked down the aisle to receive her diploma, our family was filled with pride.

But she sure couldn't pick husbands worth a darn! After divorcing my abusive father, she married a real cold fish that didn't want much to do with her four children. So, brother Bill and I (at the age of 12) went to live with Father. Not the best choice. If it wasn't for my sweet stepmother Mary, I'm not sure what would have happened. And so at 17 years of age, leaving home was easy.

If you went to college, had rich parents, or just got lucky in the draft, you just didn't go. Not so for me. Oh no, I'm the genius who hung out with the Fliss brothers. That's right, and I walked right out school halfway through my senior year at Queen Anne High School. When principal Harris sat me down in his office and said, "Lane, if you cut ONE MORE TIME!" And of course I stopped him right there and said, "Okay, let's get this over with...I Quit!"

Oh yes, and when I had pawned all I owned to get rent money, I still had my bowling ball (with my name on it) rolling around in this old Chrysler I had at the time. Yes, I was a wild one and with my friends stopped the car, got out, and rolled the ball down the steep Counter Balance road on Queen Anne Hill in Seattle. Yes, it's like one of those moments when you try to take it back and can't. Like asking the girl "How far along are you?" and she says with that glare in her eye, "I'm not pregnant."

I just stood there watching as it rolled on, and each block got faster and faster with me frozen in the middle of the street as time stood still. At the bottom of the hill waiting for the light was a two-door 1952 Chevy Cabriolet. The ball launched one more time, and I thought, "What have I done?" Somehow it hit the street just before the bumper and scrunched underneath the car, and no one was hurt. Yes, I know what you're saying. Stupid Boy!

The funny thing is, back then if you were an average white guy—pretty much me—jobs were easy to get without a high school education. So I left home and got a job at Puckett's Fish Cannery on Harbor Island—where hazardous waste and three-eyed trout are well stocked! This is thanks to Boeing and others who for years dumped PCB's and other chemicals into the soil and the Duwamish River. The average life span of anyone living in this area is seventy years, and the national average is seventy-eight!

Puckett's Fish Cannery was a gigantic concrete building with ten crews packing cans of salmon, and the noise would bounce off those concrete walls like a large echo chamber. These jobs are now all done by…oh yes, machines! The cool part was, get'er done and go home. When you would stack 100 pallets, you'd go home. So we would always get done around one or 2 P.M. instead of 3. But the fastest crew was right next to us, and they would always be done by noon or before. No matter how hard we tried, we could never be as fast as this complete crew of deaf-mute men who had no noise distractions. They seemed to be in such unison. They taught me to respect those who are different. Someone's disability should not define them, and it actually only gave us all working there greater understanding.

CHAPTER 3

I MUST SAY, I was an unwilling participant in this war and did not carry the correct attitude of a gung-ho soldier. The day I was inducted began this sordid journey.

There were protests going all over the country, but still at six o'clock in the morning, the horn honked, and the Fliss brothers were there in a 1951 Packard to pick me up. I just loved that flathead, eight-cylinder, four-door cruiser. Frank had purchased this gem of a car for three lids and a bicycle. Yes, those were the days when barter was still working. They had been up all night doing what Fliss brothers did and figured I needed counseling. Teddy Fliss was one of those people who would never do what was expected. A talented athlete, six foot three inches, and tough as nails, but of course his path led him to be Absent Without Leave (AWOL) from the marines. And he wasn't going back. So this was my adviser?

Teddy tried every way to tell me not to go, but finally with his brother Frank at the wheel, he drove us down to the induction center in Seattle. I remember looking out the window of the dreary induction center building and watching this long-haired dude so messed up on drugs actually crawl into the entrance of the center. And at the end of that day, he was not accepted and was sent home. I damn sure missed that opportunity, and me with the Fliss brothers. Go figure. I guess it was just another nineteen year-old not thinking.

So after a family farewell party, off I went on the army bus to Fort Lewis Washington, where we were to receive our basic training. Boot camp was one of the toughest things I have ever done. They knocked you down, so they could build you up, to prepare you to kill someone before they killed you!

The basic training course at Fort Lewis would eventually graduate 233,000 soldiers, with the last graduate completing training in December 1971. Today's basic training does not allow some of things they did to men back then. Drill Sergeants were allowed a full array of physical and mental punishment. I got kicked, hit, and degraded to get me ready for the worst to come. I did more pushups than I could count. Oh yeah, me and my big fat mouth! It was ten weeks of hell that left some leaving for Canada in the middle of the night, but I toughed it out and was on my way to graduation, but I ended up at Madigan hospital with an upper respiratory infection, along with seven other soldiers from our platoon. Yes, URI was caused by them having us crawl under the wire through rain, mud puddles, and CS gas (The worst).

The drill sergeant would actually make us take off our rain gear and crawl through the mud and rain, literally submerging our heads under the barbed wire, and then once done, we were to get back in formation and put our rain gear back on. It was typical military insanity!

And through it all I am still truly grateful for the experience, for it was those times that made me a man and better able to handle the things that lay ahead. Basically, if you can handle this, you can handle anything.

I also was able to get my G.E.D., the equivalent of a high school degree! I was able to take the test and was asked such questions as, "Who was our first president," and "Where is Pearl Harbor?" I know that may be a little tough for some people today, but I passed with flying colors.

Once out of the hospital, we were all back in the barracks, when we received our orders for the next transition. Talk about a nervous time, as this would tell you which type of war you were going to see. You could go to finance School, quartermaster school, engineering school, aviation logistics school or intelligence school. Certainly not any of us got those gems. Oh no, we got infantry or artillery school. When I received my orders to go to artillery at Fort Sill, Oklahoma to learn to fire howitzers, I said, "What the heck's a howitzer and how bad is this is going to be?" As it turned out, it was certainly better than infantry. So off I went to Fort Sill, Oklahoma for Advanced Individual Training (AIT) to learn to fire 155, 8-inch, and 175 millimeter howitzers from a range of 9 to 20 miles. I would tell my friends back home how to get to Fort Sill: just look for the one tree in Oklahoma and take a left!

Before leaving for AIT, however, we were given seven days leave at Christmas, and all my friends in Seattle got me a ticket to go see Creedence Clearwater Revival at Eagles Auditorium in downtown Seattle. Man, what a show. They played *Susie Q.*, *Born on the Bijou*, and *Bad Moon Rising*. With all the protests and attitudes toward the war, I sure stuck out like a proverbial sore thumb with my bald head shaved from basic training. Man, did I get the looks and double takes. That experience certainly supported my low view of the war. Yes, Bad Moon Rising.

Although the U.S. presence was rapidly dwindling, the years 1969 to 1970 saw 14,000 of the nearly 50,000 total U.S. military deaths in Vietnam. This was nearly 20 fatalities a day, compared to the approximately two per day experienced in Iraq in mid-2004. Not until 1995 did Vietnam release its official estimate of war dead: from 1955-1975, as many as 2 million civilians on both sides and some 1.1 million North Vietnamese and Viet Cong fighters. The U.S. military has estimated that between 200,000 and 250,000 South Vietnamese soldiers died in the war.

The Vietnam draft numbers are a little misleading because 90 percent of the army infantry consisted of draftees by 1969. The draft was abolished in 1973. During the Vietnam War, about two-thirds of American troops were volunteers. The rest were selected for military service through the draft. But a lot of the volunteers did so because they saw their number low in the draft and wanted to select their service, such as marine corps, coast guard, navy, or air force. Men who had physical or mental problems, were married, with children, attending college, or who were needed at home to support their families might be granted deferments.

If you stated that you were gay, you were not allowed. It is worth noting that many men who received deferments were from wealthy and educated families. Prominent political figures who avoided the draft include Bill Clinton, Joe Biden, Rudy Giuliani, Mitt Romney, and Newt Gingrich, and there is a total of five deferments each for Donald Trump and Dick Cheney. Yes Dick (MF) Cheney. As a matter of fact, American forces in Vietnam were 25 percent poor, 55 percent working-class, and 20 percent middle-class men, but very few came from upper-class families.

An interesting study conducted by the *New York Times* shows that there were 88 percent white, 11 percent black, and 1 percent other. Even though 11 percent of the total troops in Vietnam were African-Americans, only 2 percent were officers. Martin Luther King had a dream that one day the sons of former slaves and sons of slave owners would sit at the same table. That dream came true the first time on the front lines of Vietnam. This was the first time that segregation was not part of an American war.

The training at Fort Sill was easier on us, and we had time to make friends. I met five great guys, and we bonded well. We were known as the "Dirty Half Dozen." Yes, it was the six of us hanging out when there was time and learning more and more that this war was wrong and unsupported.

David O'Doud was an interesting example of the classic Californian surfer dude who has somehow lost his way. We were bunkmates in the barracks and had an exciting time while we trained on 155 Howitzers. The 155s could be towed by truck and were developed and used by the United States Army. It was first produced in 1942 as a medium artillery piece. It saw service with the U.S. Army during World War II, the Korean War, and the Vietnam War, with a total of 10,300 manufactured for war.

Back at the barracks David would smuggle booze into the barracks, and we would rock it and go into Lawton, the town off base, and cruise for the ladies. The ladies loved David and that California style. And I was always happy to get what was left over.

It was nearing the end of January 1969, and we started feeling the pressure of actually going to this unjust war. After graduating, David turned to me and said, "Lane, I want you to know I've got some connections." I always worry when somebody's got connections. He said that his sister and boyfriend were with the underground out of L.A. Yes, we're talking about people trying to help people get out of the war. Canadian immigration statistics show that 20,000 to 30,000 draft-eligible American men came to Canada as immigrants during the Vietnam era. In 1974, President Gerald Ford offered amnesty to tens of thousands of Vietnam draft dodgers and deserters.

So O'Doud said they had money and a route to get us to Canada.

I said," Yeah, if pigs could fly."

He said "No man, this is the truth, and we've got one more pass off base, and I'm going to keep going."

After careful thought, I said, "Okay I'm in, on one condition. I hope you have more than the thirty dollars in your pocket!" Yes, going AWOL. Teddy Fliss would be so proud.

As it turned out, the Dirty Half Dozen had all left at the same time, unbeknownst to us. Our other friends Mark and Jim went east, and Larry and Ed went north. Truly an amazing coincidence.

Chapter 4

THE NEXT NIGHT WE CAUGHT THE CAB to Lawton, and we just kept on going, hitchhiking through Oklahoma, Texas, New Mexico, Arizona, and all the way to Palm Springs. Yes. 1,180 weary hitchhiking miles with many interesting rides! The third ride we got was from a farmer out of southern Texas, and when we got in his pickup, he looked us over and said "You boys look like you're running away from something." With our shined shoes and our short haircuts, I guess we were pretty easy to read.

He said, "No harm boys, and I'll take you where you want to go if you listen to my fishin' story." He went on to tell us about when he was fishing the Columbia River and he had put a full chicken on a gaff hook. With the gaff hooked attached to a long rope tied to a team of horses, he threw that chicken in the river.

He'd been trying to catch this 12-foot sturgeon that weighed 1,000 pounds for many years. So then he says with a chuckle, "Yes you got it, this damned sturgeon ate the chicken and drowned both the horses."

That took him five miles past his normal turn, and we said, "Thanks for the memories, gotta go Mister." Now that's a whopper! We do love those Texas people.

Hitchhiking is either waiting or riding and not much in between, and especially in New Mexico where the sand and cactus make it look like a moon landing, but we sure loved the open spaces and dry days. David was a good companion for such a journey.

We stopped in a little town in New Mexico off of Highway 40. We were in for a night of mixing it up and letting it loose. Yes, the drinking age back then in New Mexico was 18 but we still could not vote. Congress consequently enacted the Voting Rights Act of 1970, which lowered the voting age to 18 for all federal, state, and local elections. Just a little too late for us. Then in 1984, Congress passed the National Minimum Drinking Age Act, which required states to raise their ages for purchase and public possession to 21 by October, 1986. Passing laws and Amendments back then was easy! Now Congress, if asked, couldn't pass the salt and pepper!

The Long Horn Bar caught our eye, and as we walked in we could smell the taste of old country and spilled beer. Perfect!

The bartender, a fifty-ish balding fellow said, "What will it be, boys?" We got our two beers, and we moved to the pool table where a game was going on. We put down the money for the next game. I had a talent for the game and played pretty well. They say, "You can't get good at this game without a misspent youth"

So I proceeded to run the table with a game of Nine ball for a few needed dollars, and I was getting ready to break the next game when I stepped on the foot of the big country fella who had lost to me. That was all it took. Standing up with smoke coming out of his ears and knocking his table aside, I knew for certain this was the wrong place, wrong time.

Of course, as usual, I say all the right things. "What ya think your gonna do Mister?" He surprised me with a quick straight jab to the face that had me sliding down along the pool table. He had caught me with a pretty good one, and I bounced back with a solid elbow smash to the side of his head. Hitting a man on the side of the head does so much more damage than to the front. The human brain can withstand front-to-back displacement many times better than the side-to-side displacement. Some kind of evolutionary thing! I'm guessing! So it was the elbow, a short hard blow that sent him sliding across the floor until his head hit the little table where a couple had a pitcher of beer, and they watched it dump all over him. I guess basic training had done me good. At this moment I looked at O'Doud and the gathering group of the hostiles and knew it was time to get the hell outta there. So as Willy Nelson would sing, "On the road again."

The next two days were just about traveling and sleeping, and we eventually ended up at our destination of Palm Springs, California, a sunny city where celebrities and tourists are everywhere, and we stood out like two cowboys at the opera. We were to meet O'Doud's sister to help get to Canada. O'Doud called and left a message, with no success. Then he tried his Mom, who said, "Don't you come around here, Boy," and I started to get the picture. Not sure I got the whole truth from David.

We were running out of money, and it just didn't look like we were going to get the help we needed. The first night we slept in an unlocked bread truck and froze. The next night, with still no word from Sis, we decided to use our last dollars for a warm and enjoyable stay at the Holiday Inn. Yeah, living large now!

As we settled in for the evening, I decided to go out and get some snacks, and I walked the area for about an hour. When I returned and walked up the stairs to the outside entrance of the second floor, things just didn't feel right. As I turned to open the door, there were the MPs with David handcuffed. Oh boy, this sure didn't look good, and I knew David must have made the call to turn himself in while I was out. I was then also handcuffed, and we were thrown into the MP's three-quarter-ton truck and driven off to Twenty-Nine Palms Marine Corps Base. This was definitely our darkest hour by far.

Marines in general don't have a very high opinion of army guys, and they nickname them doggies. What David and I witnessed that night in this marine brig was one of the most brutal and despicable things done by humans. My faith in man would take a nose dive.

As we arrived, we had that sense of vultures circling. There seemed to be an evil joy from the marines upon our arrival. The wickedness of their look at us was like we were their prey.

As we entered the cell we were greeted by Ray, another army detainee, who had both eyes blackened to the point that he could hardly see, and yet he was still crying for joy because he knew that he would get a night of relief from those bastards. Yes, no doubt another "Bad Moon Rising."

This was a very small jail with just one cell and the main processing room, and it reminded me of some old western jail. The brig was buzzing with the story of new meat, and everybody wanted a piece of us. They opened the cell door and took us out to the main office area and started hitting us with nightsticks on our back legs as we stood at attention. There were cigarette burns, and of course, why not throw in a little hot coffee on us as well?

Then to our surprise, the guys from the next shift came in just to enjoy a little bit of this twisted mentality, and the next shift sergeant started choking me until I nearly passed out.

As the evening went on, David and I just tried to figure out how we were going to survive this. I honestly couldn't believe that one military person could treat another with such brutal disregard for human life. The beatings started again, and at that moment I realized I had had enough. I grabbed one of the nightsticks, and for a brief moment had a victory as I took out two guys, and then things got a little blurry as they all piled on.

When I woke up on the floor, I saw that David was still taking quite a beating. They made us eat signs of cardboard, water boarded us in the toilets, and all of this went on until four o'clock in the morning. No, they were not trying to get a confession from us of some dark secret we had. It was just torture to see us bleed. It's important to note that this entire event happened with us not locked and secured in our cell. The scars of this evening have never left my memory, and I will always remember that humankind does have its evil side. Certainly, this was the end of my naive innocence! Yes, you can be sure that back then, no news got out on this story and many other incidents at this hellhole called 29 Palms Marine brig.

I'm sure some of these guys went on to work as bad policemen, shooting and abusing their power.

Amazingly, at 6 A.M., as we were bruised, bleeding, hungry, tired and confused, a young marine orderly and two MP's came into the brig and handed us our orders to fly back to Fort Sill. Hallelujah! So the whole 18 hours of abuse was for? Yes, I don't know either. I will never forget our departure with my middle finger flying high in the faces of such tyranny and curiously enough, not even in handcuffs. Yes, they just put us back in the truck and took us to the airport and then with no guard put us on the plane back to the luxury of Fort Sill, Oklahoma. I think this was when I really started swearing and using F-bombs a lot more. At least that's my excuse. Yes, I know that going AWOL is a serious offense, but this was the strangest roller coaster ride that made no sense.

Back at Fort Sill again, with the disapproving eyes of many, we were then put back in our original barracks, and imagine our surprise when we were reunited with the original dirty half-dozen. Yes, those boys all got caught or quit as well, and we were all there to be processed on what they called an Article 15. It's kind of like a misdemeanor slap on the wrist in civilian life except they deduct a great deal of your pay and bust you down from Corporal to Private. An Article 15 punishment is much lower than what a court martial could adjudge. For example, you cannot be sentenced to confinement with an Article 15 hearing. Even if found guilty at an Article 15 hearing, you still have no federal conviction, as you do with a court-martial conviction. Somehow I still had a clean record. Unbelievable!

This process took a few weeks, and we were restricted to just base only. During that time we got a chance to hang with some of the other trainees. One of these was Jerry Monet. He was on his second training course, as he failed the first one intentionally. One of the funniest and most interesting guys, Monet was another California boy with eyes that looked like they were always finding some new surprise and a mind to go with it. His technique during training was always to fall out of formation. Yes, actually he would be in formation and just fall down. I got to watch him one day as we had time on our hands standing to one side. He had that crazy look in his eye and then just fell over! I laughed so hard I almost fell myself.

He told us that there was no way we would ever see him in Vietnam. What are the odds that two months later while I was in Copperhead landing zone in Vietnam, I got a notice from our battery commander that Jerry Monet had arrived on gun five. I laughed for three days on that one, and there is no question that life could throw you some serious crazy curveballs.

I sent this postcard home to the folks to let them know what fine deluxe accommodations I was staying in. These are the typical barracks that you find in almost every military outlet throughout the country and in many foreign lands.

The morning of our departure from Fort Sill to fly to Vietnam, a car pulled up to the parking lot next to our barracks. We were literally ten minutes away to catch the bus to the airport, and to our great surprise it was David O'Dowd's sister and boyfriend, with cash and a change of clothes to take us to Canada. You what? Yes, this felt like some third grade surreal movie. David and I got in the backseat to talk with them and literally had ten minutes to decide to go to Vietnam or run! This was certainly the biggest decision of either of our young lives! So we looked at each other and I said, "After all we've been through, oh what the hell! Let's go to 'Nam." We were so beaten down from our difficult experience, we just weren't ready for any more. There were many times later I regretted that decision.

Chapter 5

WE LANDED AT BIÊN HÒA AIR BASE, located in southern Vietnam and sixteen miles east of Saigon. The massive base at Long Bihn was perhaps the largest American military base ever constructed on foreign soil. Now a vacant lot, it was a huge amalgamation of tents, buildings, and bunkers that covered hundreds of acres.

We received our orders, and I lucked out! Given a M16 and a truck ride north of Saigon, I was sent to (LZ) Landing Zone Copperhead. Some were sent as infantry into the bush, but I was heading to a secure area north of Saigon, now known as Ho Chi Minh City. To feel the heat and mugginess of this place was so stifling. Let's just say if you had a book of matches in your pocket, they wouldn't last thirty minutes before they wouldn't light! We always carried all our wallets, matches, and pictures in a plastic bag to protect them. And riding down these dusty, unpaved, narrow roads left our faces caked with mud from the sweat and dust. When the monsoon season came it was like clockwork every day. Southern Vietnam is generally dry and hot from November to April and warm and wet between May and October, with the highest rainfall in June, July, and August. That's monsoon season. If you had a bar of soap, at 5 P.M. every day you could always count on the best shower you ever had!

And the cumulus clouds that majestically climb thousands of feet always left you truly mystified at their beauty and size.

> *"We should declare war on North Vietnam…We could pave the whole country and put parking strips on it, and still be home by Christmas."*
>
> —Ronald Reagan, 1965
>
> *"You can kill ten of my men for every one I kill of yours, but even at those odds, you will lose and I will win."*
>
> —Ho Chi Minh to the French, late 1940s

I've looked back many times over the years and determined that most of our leaders at the time (Reagan, Johnson, Nixon, Ford and McNamara) really didn't know what they got into and didn't know how to get us out. As it turns out, Nixon really was the one that did get us out. "I'm not going to be the first American president to lose a war," Nixon said in October, 1969. But still that was not the case.

And yes, he was much more well known as the president who quit before he got impeached!

Chuck Hagel, Secretary of Defense in the Obama administration, volunteered to serve in the Vietnam War when he was twenty-one. He has stated: "The company commanders and the platoon leaders, they were the ones obviously on the ground with you. But I was not much impressed with our battalion leaders, our Xo's. I didn't ever get a sense that they came down in, enough into the platoon company level to really do what I thought officers should do. And some of the officers couldn't read maps very well."

Most national guard units did not go to Vietnam. Neither did most of active duty personnel. Many national guard commanders prepared for and expected activation in the early days of the war, but President Johnson decided against it. He didn't want to send a message around the world that America was actually declaring all-out war against Vietnam. And that was exactly what we saw and felt while we were there. Committed but not committed. It's trying to drive a car without the gas. I don't believe that even if Johnson had called up the national guard in large numbers, the war would still have ended as it did. Army national guard units mobilized to Vietnam included Kentucky's 2nd Battalion, 138th Artillery; Indiana's Company D (Ranger), 151st Infantry; Hawaii's 29th Infantry Brigade; Kansas' 69th Infantry Brigade; one infantry battalion from the Iowa Guard; California's 1st Squadron, 18th Armored Cavalry; New Hampshire's 3rd Battalion, 197th Artillery; and numerous engineering, postal, medical and support units. Also, many national guard members were involved in keeping the peace during so many protests in America.

New Hampshire's national guard had started to pack up and go home. They had done their time, and I was part of the gradual infusion program of personnel to take their place. The hardest part was learning to speak New Hampshire. It's kind of like trying to speak Brooklyn but a little nicer. These men were good to work and fight with and always had your back. They should be proud they served in such an admirable and honorable way.

Even today, Vietnam and its people are ever present in our lives. I was having my hair cut by a wonderful young lady who was a refugee from Vietnam. Her father was a captain in the South Vietnamese Army, and we talked about the time in 1975 when it all came to an end and the south surrendered and the peace agreement which made sure that he was somewhat protected. However, they had what they called re-education camps in which he had to spend ten years basically in a prisoner of war camp. This captain was not alone as he was in the same prison as senator John McCain, who spent 5½ years in captivity as a POW in North Vietnam.

It took 18 years for this South Vietnamese captain and his family to leave Vietnam and arrive in America where they live today around the Seattle area. It struck me that these fine people were at least well taken care of by us after our mistakes. At least America did live up to its promises.

So there I was with mud-caked face and a wet book of matches riding to LZ Copperhead, Vietnam. As we rode in, I saw the battery of six 155 Howitzers on the left. They drove us to the headquarters building to meet our commanding officer (CO) and see where we were going to be. I will say, these were some of the finest men and leaders I had run across in my fourteen months in Vietnam.

I got my orders to be on gun six. and I started to settle in with the crew. They were happy to see me, as it meant they were heading home soon.

With a total crew of 9, the 155 millimeter howitzer weighs 16,000 pounds, allowing it to be dropped by parachute or transported by a CH-53E Super Stallion or CH-47 Chinook or towed by truck. Most of Copperhead was already built and in place when I settled into my place in the bunker on gun six.

CHAPTER 6

FIRE MISSIONS CAN BE ANYTIME, when you get shaken out of bed or during the day and everyone assumes their positions on the gun and gets them ready to fire. We've got the enemy in the open and want to kick ass before the infantry comes in to finish them off. It started with the forward observer (FO) who called in the enemy position to our CO, who then sent it to our man on the radio. He gets the quadrant and deflection to pinpoint our target accurately and not hit our own soldiers on the ground. Friendly fire is so unfriendly! He calls it out to the gunner—who was usually me— who sets it. Another sets the round by adding the explosive tip to the round. Then two others set the round on a tray and bring it to the gun with the door open, and behind them is still another with the long ramming rod that pushes it into position. Then we add the charge of explosive that, once fired, shoots the round out the barrel, twisting to its destination. You can actually see the round leave the barrel. It is truly a full team effort and we needed all parts working smoothly.

One thing I remember so well was how creative the troops could be. These guys could do things in a manner that just made you stop and laugh as we were being woke up at "oh dark thirty." They created an entirely new language. One draftee woke us up to "ham and eggs on the ground," which means round HE (high explosives) with Charlie in the open.

Many different types of rounds did many different things. High explosives (HE) was set to either explode on impact or above ground, depending on the need. The bee hive round would explode just above ground, with a thousand razors going in all directions. This could cut the enemy to pieces, but stand behind a piece of plywood, and it had no effect. Willie Papa (White Phosphorous) was a crazy hot round the could burn through anything. We even had the Night Light, which provides battlefield illumination of 1 million candle power with a parachute floating above the enemy for high visibility.

My bunk-mate, a long tall drink of water named George, filled me in on my duties and what to avoid. He told me all about what his girl was like and how he missed her so. He took me under his wing and showed me the ropes to understand all the ins and outs of this camp and what not to do. He showed me how to take the malaria pills, to watch out for the black scorpions and the small snake called the "three-step viper," because one bite and three steps is all you got! It is one of the most venomous snakes in the world!

I later learned the true art of filling sandbags on those hot and muggy days. The guns were always in a sandbag-protected parapet area to protect the crew. They also helped keep incoming rockets from hitting the ammo. You can imagine a whole bunch of ninety-five-pound bombs exploding in camp. Ouch!

We would have fire missions almost every night. Sometimes twenty rounds and sometimes two hundred, we just never knew. Sleep became a thing to cherish. Sometimes we would be called to our guns for an hour and then told we were not needed. We just never knew from one night to the next.

One night the VC (Viet-Cong) guerrillas took out the kitchen with a rocket. Some of us thought it was an act of God, as the food was pretty bad, but the cooks were always quite creative with what they had to work with.

Most Vets came out of Nam weighing less than when they went in. I went in at 160 and left weighing 135 pounds. I never felt like eating or drinking beer. With the heat and mugginess it just wasn't a high priority. It's the new crash diet. Fourteen months in Vietnam. No wonder the Vietnamese were so skinny.

Now the music. Man, I still needed some music. I was into Hendrix, Richie Havens, Credence and the Almond Brothers, so I had my friends send me over those LP's. Yes, still no cassettes at that time. I had a portable, battery-operated record player that worked some of the time. Just hungry for any sound! Anything was better than the Armed Forces radio. Their music was old swing and Richard Nixon would come on for support. Really Tricky Dick? Of course still better than listening to Hanoi Hanna, the North Vietnamese propaganda station. which would start the show off with "How are you, GI Joe? It seems to me that most of you are poorly informed about the way the war is going. Nothing is more confusing than to be ordered into a war to die or to be maimed for life without the faintest idea of what's going on." Then she would play some anti-war songs like Barry McGuire's *Eve of Destruction*, Bob Dylan's *Blowing In the Wind*, and Country Joe and the Fish's *Vietnam War Song*, which was played at Woodstock 1969. I sure enough missed that show!

The pot they had, that definitely helped my appetite. Mama-san would call it gonge, dinky-dow stick, and she was right. Wow! (Dinky Dow is a bastardization of the Vietnamese dien cai dau, meaning bat shit crazy) We would use it sparingly however. because you never knew when the next fire fight would be.

One night in the monsoon season, I was sitting on the rail, setting quadrant deflection (getting the barrel in exactly the right spot to fire), and it was raining and muddy as hell. We fired, and the whole gun went up on its two back legs like a bucking bronc, and I rode that thing yelling all the way down. From that moment on, I had my nickname, Jesse James. So Jesse was the gunner for gun six, and I kinda took it to heart. No, I did not go and get a cowboy hat at the store. What store!

The next day we dug trenches and installed heavy beams that looked like railroad ties and drove spikes into them to hold them. This would secure the blades in the mud, so I wouldn't go riding like that again!

Our Sergeant Johnson typified that east coast New Hampshire arrogance and was a little rough around the edges but was a good man who took care of his people. One day he was giving Momma Son (A Vietnamese woman who did some work for us) a bad time. She stopped what she was doing, turned to him and said "No sweat GI, me number one when I die."

These were surely some beautiful people in the middle of hell's kitchen! The Vietnamese people were always kind and helpful to us. On one hot and muggy day as we were driving back to camp, we went by the dump where we got rid of our garbage, and there was mama son rummaging through maggot-infested chicken to take home to her children. Eighty percent of South Vietnam was rural and poor. Some GI's treated them with great disdain and physical harm.

So many times I've heard the stories of one GI shooting a family's water buffalo for sport, which made it damn near impossible for them to farm their rice. To think that over those ten years these kind innocent people were killed at such a rapid rate. Yes, more than one million civilians were killed in this war.

And while driving, coming alongside a Vietnamese bicyclist, some would bump them off into the ditch by yanking the wheel of their truck. There should have been a law against our American arrogance.

Jerry Monet (my California buddy from Fort Sill) and I spent a lot of good times together doing night guard duty and talking about the things we wanted to do when we got home. I can't tell you how many times we heard the thunderous roar that would rattle us to the core and bring dust out of the bunkers from the B-52 bombers' continuous bombing runs, which made craters the size of houses. Tanks had to be careful not to drop into one of those.

On another rainy night, we were firing two rounds per minute, with one guy setting the projectile, with many different settings. In this case, it was round (HE) for high explosive once it hits its target. Inside the tip of the artillery shell there are three centrifugal force trigger mechanisms, so as the rounds twists in the air, all three go off, and that puts the round ready for impact and explosion.

On this particular night, we would always have a metal shell holder with one man on each side to hold this ninety-five-pound shell. Larry, who was closest to me, tripped and the shell slid out and hit the ground. That moment of shock and then…all of us trying to get the hell out of the way. Lucky for us, once we took the cap off, only two out of the three firing pins had gone off. Moments like these are when even atheists thank God.

The first six months at Copperhead were the easiest of my tour. We didn't lose a single guy during that period of time, especially with the mandate that the New Hampshire guard was not to be put in harm's way. Believe it or not, we were even able to play a game of volleyball. When the higher-ups saw this to be a good thing, we were then ordered to fly to the South Vietnamese soldiers camps to compete in three games and then have a major feast of monkey, snake, and God-knows-what other foods. It was great and delicious, and it was wonderful to unify the American troops with the South Vietnamese. So on four or five occasions, we were flown in to many different regions of South Vietnam to play volleyball. Also, the South Vietnamese soldiers would come to Copperhead and compete against us.

On the last of these competitions before the New Hampshire Guard was sent home, we had a terrific battle against the Vietnamese soldiers. We had each won a match, and going into the last game everybody was into it, and they had a six-foot four-inch jumper who could blow it right through our hands. He probably could have been an Olympic medalist, and I learned as we lost that match that white guys really can't jump.

Near the end of our stay at Copperhead, rainfall had become extreme, and we had small ponds, which were now very large and needed to be removed. So they brought in the army corps of engineers with bulldozers to push the water out. These three bulldozers would start at one side, put their blades down, and go through these ponds, and we watched the multitudes of reptiles jumping and leaping in desperation in front to stay away from the blades. Frogs, snakes, leeches, and lizards, of all types. Truly an amazing and disturbing sight.

They called it the saddest day in Manchester's history, September 9th, 1969, the late summer day when five of the city's sons were killed by the same land mine in Vietnam as they prepared to head home. They were returned in flag-draped coffins. A few days later, the rest of their national guard unit arrived home to a different, but equally emotional welcome. "We cried at both," said former guardsman Roland Provencher of Manchester, whose best friend was one of the five guardsmen killed on Aug. 26, 1969. "It was a very sad and a very happy time." New Hampshire's 3rd Battalion, 197th Artillery, went to Vietnam in 1968, becoming one of the first of a handful of national guard units to go.

But the deaths of the five Manchester guardsmen, killed by a land mine as they rode in the back of a truck after surviving a year in Vietnam, shocked the city and state and brought home the meaning of war.

> *"Two thousand people jammed Manchester's small airport when the bodies arrived on August 30th. The sound of drums helped provoke such grief that the drummer stopped playing. Then-mayor John Mongan called it 'the saddest day for Manchester that I can remember.'"*
>
> —David Tirrell-Wysocki, Associated Press Writer

CHAPTER 7

MORE REGULAR ARMY TROOPS continued to be infused into our camp as the New Hampshire guard continued to go home.

Once this was completed, we were then sent to fire base Quan Loi, sixty miles north of Saigon and ten miles from the Cambodian border. It was originally a village drawing life from a French rubber plantation in the highlands of northern Three Corps near An Loc and was characterized by its red soil. Everyone back in the U.S. who read my letters saw envelopes smudged with dirty rouge from the red clay, painted into the paper by sweaty hands that were sticky with perspiration almost constantly. The soil must have been good for rubber trees, since the plantation was the reason for Quan Loi's existence. Quan Loi was a part of the Terra Rouge (red land) Rubber Company. Michelin plantation was some miles to the south.

The road from Copperhead to Quan Loi was called Thunder Road, and for good reason. Twice we were stopped with mortar fire and rocket fire, and we lost one vehicle, and when the bullets peppered our truck, we knew the shit was hitting the fan. I was thinking how I had just signed my extension for two extra months in Vietnam so I could go home and be out of the army. My

F-bombs were flying again. I don't think the ink was dry when this all came down. We lost two good men that day.

Arriving in Quan Loi, we set our six guns into position and started filling sandbags for bunkers and also for the parapets to protect our 155's. Every gun crew could go ahead and design what we wanted, and ours was long and straight with sandbags on all sides, and on top was corrugated steel and then more sandbags all the way across the roof. Most bunkers were built similar to this one and you know we were in a hurry to get it done, as Charlie (VC) was just around the corner.

In Iraq they developed a new system; they call it the "bunker kit," which can be filled and set up much faster than traditional sandbags and has become a popular security device among U.S. forces in Iraq. But you better have a bucket loader, and it just doesn't work in the boonies.

One night on guard duty in the middle of a ground attack, I was operating a fifty cal machine gun with tracers every five bullets so I could watch the path of the bullets. I shot a zapper through the wire, grazing his side, and he didn't go down. God did I miss him? He was so doped up it took two hits before he went down. And another one right behind him!

Later when we had their bodies in the yard for inspection, we discovered they were carrying three or four different packets of heroin, opium, and speed. These guys obviously knew they were going down, and I could see that the enemy was so willing to die for his country. This is when I began to realize how tough this was going to be against such a strong opposing force.

> **Tracer ammunition** are bullets or cannon caliber projectiles that are built with a small pyrotechnic charge in their base. Ignited by the burning powder, the pyrotechnic composition burns very brightly, making the projectile trajectory visible to the naked eye during daylight and very bright during nighttime firing. This enables the shooter to make aiming corrections without observing the impact of the rounds fired and without using the sights of the weapon.

On another warm and quiet evening I was on guard duty again, and as I looked across the valley where the rows of rubber trees were, in the darkness I saw a single bright light swinging back and forth on a tree limb. It was an eerie sight just silently swinging. Our reaction from across the valley was to blow the hell out of it, and of course Charlie was laughing at us. It was just another trick to understand and pinpoint the exact location of every firing bunker and howitzer. I have a lot of respect for those guerrillas who wanted their land back and literally would do anything at any cost.

These guys would mess with your head. On one occasion, we were near the Black Virgin Mountain near Tay Ninh, and as the morning progressed we heard the noise of trucks running three quarters up the mountain. As we looked toward the noise, we saw a U.S. Army Jeep and a three-quarter-ton truck driving along. Can you imagine our shock at how they could steal our trucks and get them up there? Again, our reaction was to throw every possible thing we could at them with airstrikes and our ground weapons.

For three hours we just blew the hell out of the side of that mountain. Moments went by and the dust cleared, and I'll be damned if we didn't hear the Jeep running along the side of the mountain again! Nothing demoralizes you more than that kind of determination, and they had such an incredible network of tunnels that ran so deep inside that mountain.

I was told that the 7th North Vietnamese Army had finally been rooted out of one area when U.S. forces found their underground headquarters. Yes, 10,000 square feet of a fine underground facility near Quan Loi, with carpets, ping-pong tables, water, and lights.

"And the rockets' red glare, the bombs bursting in air." This took on a totally different meaning for me. The amount of times I dove in a place of protection to get away from rockets was past counting. It became like a ritual or routine. Being sitting ducks on bases and LZ's always left us vulnerable.

And if that is not bad enough, our guys would CS gas the enemy, and the wind would blow it back to us so many times we became immune to the stuff. That, I never thought could be possible, but I guess we can get used to anything. Thank God we didn't experience a lot of Agent Orange. It did its damage to so many after Nam.

I do understand that we were there to help the South against the northern invaders. But imagine just once, to think we had a foreign country encamped in our land. We cannot grasp that concept, but if it were to come about, then you like so many would fight to the death to keep your land and country!

Chapter 8

When we had moved to Quan Loi, we had new leadership, and it was a sad and sorry lot. We could always make light of the next stupid thing our captain or colonels would do. And they, like so many, were just career army and made it up the ranks simply by doing their time. We called them lifers.

Our Captain Forsythe was a tall, goofy looking Baby Huey type that was always sucking up to the colonel and showing little regard for his troops. Nicknamed Captain Dickhead, he was one of those guys that went through the process of being an officer who truly had no character, no honor, and no ability to lead men. All he had was the diligence to not screw up stateside. But put his kind in real situations, in real time, and this is where the army really had no clue. When we moved into Quan Loi, he was the first to build his bunkers, and of course he put his underground for the best protection. Four nights in a row at 4:30 we would receive rocket fire exploding all over the base and a number on our battery.

On the 5th day this SOB chose that same exact time to have us do police call (picking up the area for trash and cigarette butts) because the colonel was coming the next day.

"What the hell?" I said. This was my final straw with this awful man. So off we went to do this stupid duty when the rockets hit us again! Everyone dove for their bunkers but me. I will never forget that surreal moment as I casually walked back not caring what happened. To be filled with such hopelessness, I could not take this anymore! The angels must have been watching over me. The guys were peeking out yelling to get me back in the bunker, and shrapnel was buzzing by my head. It was like a slow-motion movie as I was grabbed by the boys who drug me into the bunker. I had some choice words for Captain Dickhead.

I had been promoted to sergeant of gun six, but then with my choice of words I used to the captain after the police call event, I was busted back down to corporal. To care for your crew and protect them from the captain was my mission, and I failed when my outburst and emotions got the best of me. I still say I'm sorry to this day! But we always had, "It don't mean nothin," and that was what got us through.

When we were out on another LZ and the general was coming in for inspection, our captain made his biggest mistake. He had the chopper with the general and colonel landing on the north side of the LZ, but they came down on the south side. To watch this panic-stricken goofball run across our compound with the look in his eyes of a scared dipstick and then fall into a mud puddle was more than we could bear. To see your leader behave like a frightened coward left us with such disillusionment and despair. We needed him to be composed and always have our backs. Certainly not this guy!

A week later one of our guys, Robert on gun four, was found outside the wire in the dump with just his shorts on, babbling in his gas mask. He was sent home and discharged with a mental breakdown (called a section 8). A lot of this was blamed on our fearless leader, Captain Dickhead!

Late one evening a few of the boys decided to make a point and went down into the underground bunker and hit Captain Dickhead with two different canisters of gas. This is called "fracking." One was a yellow smoke grenade that left him yellow for several days, and the other was CS gas, which just makes your face scream in agony. It's like being poked in both eyes while someone is lighting your face on fire. I can just say he got only half of what he deserved. There were many accounts of our colonel and others who had a bounty on them. Ours was eventually killed, and the perpetrator was never identified.

My friendship with Jerry Monet had been great throughout the war, and we always found time to hang out; it was one of the great things that came of this bloody mess.

One slow night, Jerry was wondering, "Hey Lane, what would it be like to just put the full charge 7 in the 155 with no shell and see what it does. These are the charges that will shoot the shells, and a charge 7 is the full amount. It's about the size and length of two loaves of bread and makes a whole lotta boom!

I said, "You be crazy, Jerry." But we both knew that. He talked of it all the time. And sure enough, when I got back from a mission with the 11th Armored Cavalry Regiment the place was all buzzing about Jerry. Yes, he had finally done it. A giant fire ball went across the sky that he said was so beautiful until it landed. Yes, it landed on the only little shack out there, and this was the place where all the guys got their marijuana and hash! All the boys were a little pissed at him, and the colonel couldn't figure out whether to bust him or give him a medal. But Jerry got his dream, and we laughed every time it came up. Good 'ole Jerry.

CHAPTER 9

THE 11ᵀᴴ ARMORED CALVARY REGIMENT provided defense for Quan Loi. Colonel George S. Patton IV commanded the 11th, just like his father before him in World War II. After his promotion to Colonel in April, 1968, he was given command of the 11th Armored Cavalry Regiment. During his three tours in Vietnam, Patton, who frequently used helicopters as a mobile command post, was shot down three times and was awarded the Distinguished Flying Cross.

After Vietnam, he was promoted to Brigadier General in June, 1970 before becoming the commanding officer of the U.S. 2nd Armored Division in 1975, as a Major General. This was a unit his father had commanded just before the U.S. had entered World War II, making this the first time in U.S. Army history that a father and son had both commanded the same division.

It was so amazing to be kicking ass riding in these killing machines and have George Patton Jr. just above us taking care of his boys. We had the sense we were being led by the best and worked hard for his admiration and support. Daily we would be rolling on a mission to protect Quan Loi at all costs and then find a clearing with all the Sherman tanks and APC's (Armored Personnel

Carriers). They would sit in a big circle for the night. This was a well-run, good bunch who knew what they were doing.

As it got dark, at whatever predetermined time we would do the "Mad Minute." Basically we would throw everything we got at the jungle to let Charlie know we mean business. It was just an incredible sound that is held deep in my memory. One minute of fury like you have never heard! While on this mission, I was assigned to assist and coordinate the air and ground attacks. Basically, have no one injured from friendly fire. "Let's keep them safe," the colonel would say.

If we got the notice for North Vietnamese or Charlie in the open, we needed a coordinated attack. So first it was air strikes, then shelling from batteries if needed, and then the ground soldiers. The problem was, we also had to, believe it or not, get approval from the provincial chiefs. Man, did we think this was bullshit, and half the time Charlie was gone by the time we got it cleared!

While preparing for one of those evenings, I fell down between two Sherman tanks and dislocated my left shoulder. The shoulder had been a problem when I was back home playing sandlot football, but nothing like this. You must understand the pain and joy of a dislocated shoulder.

When it's out, your body can't handle the pain, so its' major shock time, and then when it goes back in! Wow! The absence of pain is nirvana! So I was able to get it back into place, and the next morning they shipped me out to the Long Bihn hospital. I'm thinking, "Okay, maybe a little R&R or maybe heading home is in my future." Foolish me! Not a chance.

They looked me over and said, "It looks fine and just a little sore." But you see, we really need to see it out of the socket.

The doctor said, "Okay, so you just head back to camp, and the next time this dislocates, if you could please just leave it out of socket until you get back here."

Just leave it out! Are you kidding! I could see me getting thrown in the brig for striking an officer. So you want me to be in excruciating pain for eight hours while I try to get down here so you can put it back in?

This thirty-five-year-old librarian looking knothead said, "Yeah I think that's what you need to do." The guy creeped me out, like Gary Cole playing Bill Lumbergh in the movie *Office Space*. I was gonna hit him with a "red stapler," and I realized this must be just a bad movie. So I stomped out and went back to Quan Loi base.

Throughout the rest of my tour, that shoulder dislocated three more times, and once it was in the middle of a pretty serious firefight. No, I did not leave it out—and miss nirvana? I became pretty good at putting it back in. Desperate times makes you think on your feet or fall. Little did I know that these dislocations would pay off in the long run when I got home. I was to be 20 percent disabled with free V.A. health care.

Later on, Jerry and I had a chance to go to Saigon and not drive down that damn Thunder Road filled with dust, bombs, and snipers. Vietnam was 80 percent rural, with absolutely no paved roads. We were hooking a ride with a Chinook helicopter. Those are the big huge twin prop beasts that haul so much and are certainly still used today.

We were hitching up our backpacks and walking along the tarmac to get in the back end of the Chinook with the ramp down, and I turned to Jerry in one of those moments when he was yakking up a storm and told him to shut the hell up. He turned around and hit me with a good one that knocked me right on my butt! Half shocked and half hurt, I proceeded to get up and give him a good one that knocked him on his rear. He got up laughing and as I helped him up, we both went arm in arm like two guys in a John Wayne movie up into the Chinook. These were crazy times for crazy people.

Saigon was amazing, with its busy streets and people everywhere. So many bicycles and scooters. And of course, we were looking for girls.

We walked into one bar, and the girl asks "Hey G.I., want to buy me a Saigon Tea? So we sit down with two girls, and we get the bill for a little shot glass of Coca-Cola. It was five dollars; yikes.

My girl then asked me to go up to her room, which I was eager to do. She was a lovely twenty-two-year-old Vietnamese girl who could speak some broken English. When we got to the room, she rather abruptly asked me to please take a shower, and I cautiously said okay, and she pointed where I should put my clothes.

So I took off my clothes and my forty-five handgun I was carrying and stacked it with my wallet and shirts and pants. The shower was just one square room with the door from the living room into it. Kind of strange that I went in to take a shower like a fool, and as soon as I was in I heard the door lock.

My first thought was "Oh my God, she's going to shoot through the door and kill me," and my second was what a damned fool I had been. Curiously enough I looked up in this shower for any place to hide and saw this short wall on one side that only went two-thirds of the way up and left a shelf I could leap up and literally go into another apartment.

Yes, sitting up on this ledge with the shower running, naked, unnerved, and not sure whether to jump into the other apartment or wait to see what happened. Minutes went by and no bullets came through the door, and I was starting to wonder if she had just stolen my money and my gun and was on the run.

To my surprise, she unlocked the door, and she peeked in and saw no one in the shower. When she looked up, her eyes were as wide as saucers as she said "You crazy G.I., what are you doing up there?"

I jumped back down and went directly to my clothes, counted the money, and grabbed the gun, and said "Girl, you're the crazy one."

Jumping down two stairs at time and checking my back, I got the hell out of there as fast as I possibly could. Some serious stupid crazy shit going down.

I met Jerry out in the street later on and said, "Hey Man, let's do anything but this!" So we decided to have a little tourist time. We got some drinks and we went for a three-wheeled motor scooter cab ride through Saigon.

This vehicle was like something out of *Casablanca*, with the driver with his safari hat, and the two wheels that were in the front, with the seat between the two front wheels, so basically if we hit anything, the bumpers were our legs and our teeth. But with enough booze in us, we got brave enough and cruised around town and had a great time, even ending up at the zoo.

We told Popa Son to wait there for us as we went sightseeing in the Saigon Zoo. The zoo turned out to be not one of your fine tourist attractions. A sadder group of animals I had not seen. Even the Vietnam dogs, who were more for dinner than pets, were still looking better than those animals.

Chapter 10

THE BOEING CH-47 CHINOOK, one of the heaviest lifting helicopters, was named after the American Indian tribe in Washington State. These were first built in 1956 and became one of the most used helicopters in Vietnam, and with many upgrades throughout the decades, it is still being used in the Middle East and wherever needed.

I was given many different jobs in Vietnam. I am not sure if that was because of my talent or my propensity to get in trouble, but one of the craziest was loading these Chinook's from underneath. Picture a large amount of ammo and bombs in a pile with the net wrapped around it and a pickup line with the loop at the top. Now I would be standing on top of this. Are you kidding me? Yes, I was standing on top of this pile of bombs waiting for the Chinook to come down and for me to attach this sortie pile to the hook that was approximately eight feet below the bottom of the helicopter. Dust, rocks, and dirt were flying everywhere as the helicopter came down, and my task was to… What? Hook this up and get off! Are you kidding me? On two occasions it was either jump off or get squished.

I think the burnout rate was pretty quick on this job, so after a week or so they had somebody else doing it, and I went back to my gun. I'm sure they must have a better method today than this.

And several days later I happened to be in our compound, and I looked up and I saw the strangest flight of the Chinook above us. Approximately six hundred feet above us, this Chinook was twisting and turning and fighting within itself. Apparently they had loaded too much, and the weight had caused the stabilizers to keep the two propellers unified, and it was basically tearing itself apart. The moment when it split in two and all the soldiers fell out was one of the more tragic moments I saw. The forward section crashed to the ground, but the rear section continued to fly around in a rather morbid salute for a few minutes, and then it also crashed. It took me and Jerry a long time before we flew on another Chinook.

When we had time to hang out, sometimes we were altogether and sometimes it was the whites in one set and the brothers in another group. One particular night we were all together, and some of us had smoked some weed. After a while I saw everyone asleep and immediately thought, Gas attack! Gas Attack!

Yes, we were told to watch for drowsiness, for that could be a sign, as you may not smell the nerve gas coming. Yes, this stuff is bad. So I held my breath and ran back to my bunker, got the atropine syringe, and stuck it in my leg. Yes, this stuff is supposed to stop the effect of nerve gas.

Symptoms of Sarin and other nerve agents include foaming at the mouth, loss of consciousness, a slow heart rate, slow breathing, vomiting, muscles spasms, and then death. Death by nerve gas is an ugly way to go.

When the residents of Khan Sheikhoun, a small village in western Syria, woke up on the morning of April 4, 2017, they had no idea what lay in store for them. Just before 17 A.M., planes dropped bombs on the town, and shortly thereafter, observers watched from the distance as a cloud of gas covered the town. It was clear that these were not conventional bombs. Ninety-two people died a terrible death from nerve gas. There is a reason Sarin gas is banned throughout the world.

Back in the bunker, I then put on my flak jacket, helmet, and gun and was ready for what I was sure was going to be a ground attack, resulting in most of our guys dead. I thought it was surely the end of it all! I was completely by myself waiting…waiting. And then I heard a sound. Yes, it was the glorious sound of guys in the next bunker playing cards. To hear "Come on Jim, your turn to deal," was when I knew I had been just tripping. Imagine the poker players when they saw me coming in their bunker in full combat gear, and they said "What the hell?" I tried to tell them what had happened, but the atropine was so strong it made my tongue all dried up, and I sounded like someone drunk or ready for the nut house! George Costanza from Seinfeld should play this part!

We had orders and were back out on another LZ, filling sandbags and getting ready for God-knows-what. And then we were informed that there was going to be a musical show that day at two o'clock. The Armed Forces Entertainment was coming to our area to provide American entertainment with priority to remote and isolated locations, such as our landing zone. This is different from the non-government United Service Organizations (USO), whose entertainers tend to be famous and generally aren't sent as close to the front line.

So it was time to hear some music, and imagine our disappointment when they brought a Vietnamese band that sang with an accent. "Hey Yoode, don make it baahhd." Yes, that was the Beatles' Hey Jude, and we were so let down.

I was not going to let this go. Yes, we were pissed, so when they took their break, myself and other soldiers jumped on stage and got the boys rolling. Our guitar player played Jimmy Hendrix'm Hey Joe, and I did Iron Butterfly's *In-A-Gadda-Da-Vida* drum solo and got a standing ovation. We may have not been all that good, but these guys were so in need of anything American, it got them rockin'!

The rats were a special breed in Nam. They were large and unafraid, especially at night. They would get in some of the guy's weed that was stored in the sand bags. After that, the rats would go a little nuts. I had one chewing on my toe and one morning woke with one siting on my forehead just looking at me. From that time forward, mosquito nets were as much to keep the rats out as mosquitos.

The army does supply rodent traps, and we got one. The trap was a square wire cage with a trap door. About every two weeks we would set the trap and catch one. It was time to educate the rats. Standing in the open between all the guns, I would get out the lighter fluid and light the rat on fire, open the door, and watch him run across the area until he died. This method gave us two weeks of peace from those buggers, and then they would start being a problem again. The rats have a two-week memory. It seems to be about what we have when it comes to foreign wars!

When Americans remember Vietnam, we often think of the war as having three major actors: the North Vietnamese, the South Vietnamese, and the American military. But there was another player: the mountain yards.

By the time the hostilities between North and South Vietnam ceased, around 200,000 mountain yards had been killed and 85 percent of their villages leveled. The Vietnamese tribesmen who fought alongside American Special Forces won the Green Berets' admiration—and lost everything else. The term Montagnard means "people of the mountain" in French and is a carry-over from the French colonial period in Vietnam. In the Vietnamese language, they are known as the "highlanders," and they fought alongside U.S. and South Vietnamese troops throughout the war.

I traded my canteen with one of my Mountain Yard buddies for a crossbow to shoot the rats. All the guys in my bunker were more scared of me than the rats and told me, "The crossbow ain't going to work."

> "Ground attack" is a word that still makes me quiver and quake with fear. Charlie running through the wire with bombs strapped to their backs, wanting to blow us up, and he didn't mind dying. They were called "sappers".
>
> The intruders, from the 2nd Company of the 409th NVA Main Force Sapper Battalion, crouched low in three-man and six-man teams, and silently slipped through the barbed wire that marked the fire base's outer defenses. Under an umbrella of NVA mortar fire, the sappers raced through the compound, tossing gas grenades and canvas satchels loaded with explosives. They then directed automatic weapons fire at the demolished or burning targets. The infiltrators hit the battalion tactical operations center and C Company's command bunker, killing Captain Richard V. Knight, the company's leader. Grunts were

> shot down trying to escape their quarters or buried alive when enemy explosives were hurled into their hooches. The base "was a shambles…with things burning all over the place," wrote the America One commander, Major General James L. Baldwin, in a letter to his family. After one hour of close-quarter combat, thirty Americans were dead and eighty-two wounded. A count of the enemy dead showed fifteen NVA bodies in and around the camp.
>
> "The attack was a stark example of the effectiveness of the sapper force. The sappers who so devastatingly struck fire base Mary Ann—as well as hundreds of minor outposts, major bases, airfields, fortified hamlets and large cities throughout South Vietnam—were members of the Bo Doi Dac Cong (roughly translated "soldiers in special forces"), a highly organized, well-trained and well-equipped organization that carried out special operations (HistoryNet).

Sappers. Yes, these guys gave today's terrorist their first lessons. When the attacks happened, all hell broke loose. With rockets exploding around us, we would be firing direct fire through the wire with our 155's. With the barrel level to the ground, as the shells exploded after every round we dove to miss being hit by our own shrapnel! You could hear it whizzing by our heads and then we would load another round.

CHAPTER 11

THE BLACK RIVERS OF VIETNAM were strange and hard to understand. How could these be waterways? Every time we got near one, we just could not understand how it could be so black. And as it turns out, both Vietnam and China have the same problem. Just absolutely no process of law and public awareness to stop anyone and any business from dumping all waste into these rivers. It was so bad and the water pollution was so clearly visible, we could see the dark black color and smell the pungent odor. One Japanese cargo ship refused to dock at Go Dau Port on the Thi Vai River because the water would corrode the ship's hull.

China today has asked its people to identify these polluted rivers and called it the "Black Stinky River Program (hi chou he). Yes that's the name of this program! So far 2,900 rivers have been discovered that are so polluted they are completely unusable, and China is in the beginnings of starting an ecological transformation of these waterways.

The days when the grunts (infantry) would come into camp for R&R at Quan Loi, R&R were so good they named a drink after it! Seeing those boys, I knew who had it the toughest. That thousand-yard stare, with eyes that said it all. That quiet look of sadness and disbelief left you knowing they had seen the worst, and we always gave them a wide berth. They needed time to get it together and readjust.

Some of my friends who came back took forty years to readjust and are still fighting in their sleep. One friend received help just recently. He started talking it through at some VA sessions, and he has grown and become the poster child for "it's never too late."

PTSD is now a common acronym. PTSD, or post-traumatic stress disorder, leapt to the public's consciousness when the American Psychiatric Association added the health issue to its diagnostic manual of mental disorders in the 1980s. But PTSD—known to previous generations as shell shock, soldier's heart, combat fatigue, or war neurosis—has roots stretching back centuries and was widely known during ancient times (History.com).

During all those years, the common treatment was, "Deal with it, Soldier." For all of us coming home, we had a lot of baggage, many things effecting us, and all were difficult. Dealing with no support, no respect, the confusion of not even knowing what was eating at us (PTSD), and adjusting to living stateside was one hell of a load!

Some would do a second and a third tour just because the adjustment stateside was more difficult to deal with than going back to that hellhole. Really? Yes, that bad.

Approximately 2,594 million U.S. serviceman served in Nam. 1,736 million army, 301,000 U.S. Marines and 293,000 U.S. Airmen (uswardogs.org).

Here are some of the Vietnam Memorial Wall facts and a little history most people will never know: There are 58,267 names now listed on that polished black wall, and the names are arranged in the order in which they were taken from us by date, and within each date the names are in alphabetical order.

There are three sets of fathers and sons on the wall. Of the names, 39,996 were just 22 or younger, and 8,283 were just 19 years-old. The largest age group, 33,103, were 18 years-old. Twelve soldiers on the wall were 17 years-old, and 997 soldiers were killed on their first day in Vietnam and 1,448 were killed on their last day in Vietnam.

So, finally my days were getting short. I had done a full year and was now wanting the next two months to be as safe as I could make them. To understand the mindset of all of us together, we knew this was an exercise going nowhere, and we were just trying to help ourselves and others until we got the hell out of here. And yes, that was self-defeating in itself! It was like a fire at a theater with everyone just trying to get out!

So of course, given my usual good fortune, I got orders to be back out in the boonies on another LZ with Captain Dickhead, who was bound to kill us all. Oh perfect! I was now one of the short-timers who walked with a little swagger. Funny how you get when your time is short. I was on guard duty with a new greenie who had been in country maybe a week, and he had the brilliant idea to take a hand grenade apart.

Yes, I thought, "What the hell is wrong with you, you stupid #%$&*@**? What are you thinking?"

I turned the fifty-caliber machine gun on him and told him to "Move off pilgrim" and take that damn grenade with you! I'd rather pull guard duty by myself than always be watching my back.

My teeth were giving me grief on the LZ, so I went to the medic and was air lifted back to Quan Loi. Hallelujah! The hot weather and a lot of Coca Colas had done my teeth in. They had one dentist there who liked to smoke hash, so I supplied him with hash, and I was able to start what turned out to be an extensive amount of tooth repair. Two months' worth! Bad teeth were saving my butt and keeping me on the base until I could go home.

When it was my time to leave, I was flown in a Chinook, and I made damn sure we were not carrying any heavy loads! The memory of those guys falling when the Chinook split in two was still too fresh!

And just as I was leaving Vietnam, President Nixon announced the new attack on Cambodia. On April 30th 1970, President Richard Nixon declared to a television audience that the U.S. military troops, accompanied by the South Vietnamese People's Army, were to invade Cambodia to disrupt the supply lines of the North.

All of our battalion went inside Cambodia to bring fire support, and so many never came home. After the first week of operations, additional battalion and brigade units were committed to the operation, so between May 6th to May 24th, a total of 90,000 Allied troops (including 33 U.S. maneuver battalions) were conducting operations inside Cambodia. Due to increasing protests in the U.S., President Nixon issued a directive on May 7th limiting the distance and duration of U.S. operations to a depth of 30 kilometers (19 mi) and setting a deadline of June 30th to get the hell out. Not exactly a fully thought out plan. During that time, over 150,000 civilians were killed.

In 1970, Prince Sihanouk of Cambodia was ousted, not by Pol Pot, but by a U.S.-backed, right-wing military coup. That same year, the U.S. invaded Cambodia to expel the North Vietnamese from their border encampments, but instead they drove them deeper into Cambodia, where they allied themselves with the Khmer Rouge. In 1975, Pol Pot had taken over Cambodia and prosecuted all the educated and started the genocide of over two million of his people. This was known as the "Killing Fields." And who was to stop this? Certainly not America, just trying to get out. In 1978, Vietnam as a whole country then attacked Cambodia, deposed Pol Pot, and re-established order in that country. It may still be one of the poorest countries in the world, but it took Vietnam to help them find the peace.

No matter what we did in Vietnam, it seems we were just strangers in a strange land.

John, our radio man on gun six, came to see me three months later in Seattle to let me know how bad it got. He was so saddened by the losses, and he also had become hooked on heroin. The Vietnamese had so many different drugs to sell and eventually found heroin as a big seller. It seemed the longer I was there the more drugs became accessible.

This beautiful land with its stunning landscapes and jungles, with its kind and gentle people, and the centuries of occupation by so many foreign aggressors. First it was the Chinese from 111 B.C. to 938 A.D. Then the Ming Dynasty 400 years later, with its continuous control and economic iron fist on people of Vietnam. No country weighs on Vietnam like China, and it has been that way for centuries. Even in 1979, China again attacked the North and 50,000 Vietnamese died. At least 200,000 Chinese troops poured into Northern Vietnam all along the border. China was aiming to punish Vietnam for its invasion of Cambodia the month before in an attempt to oust the Chinese-backed Khmer Rouge. This seemed so odd, as Pol Pot had killed so many. These folks just can't cut a break, and if asked, most in Vietnam still think the French and American occupations were short compared to the Chinese.

In 1846, the French, authorized by Napoleon, launched a naval expedition to punish and force Vietnam to accept French protectorate after several missionaries had been killed. By 1861, France and Vietnam signed the Treaty of Saigon and the French had taken control of all South Vietnam. Continuing its control, in 1893 France occupied all of Vietnam, Cambodia and Laos, until 1954.

Hours after the end of World War II, Ho Chi Minh declared the independence of Vietnam from France. and the collapse of Vietnam's monarchy. France attempted to re-establish its colonial rule but was ultimately defeated in 1954 in the First Indochina War. Vietnam was then divided into northern and southern regions, with Ho Chi Minh in command of North Vietnam and Emperor Bao Dai in control of South Vietnam.

Although I don't believe in Ho Chi Mihn's ideology, he was a strong and long-lasting leader. Born in 1890, he traveled the world and lived in Paris, London, Moscow, and even in the U.S. On the 4th of August, 1914, the night World War I began, Churchill dined with Lloyd George at the Carlton Hotel, where Ho Chi Minh was employed as a cook. This guy really got around!

> Ho went on to become the leader of North Vietnam, and in 1966 he was asked if he would fight to final victory, Minh stated, "If by 'final victory' you mean the departure of the Americans, then we will fight to final victory. Everything depends on the Americans. If they want to make war for twenty years, then we shall make war for twenty years. If they want to make peace, we shall make peace and invite them to tea afterwards."
>
> He died in 1969, six years before the North declared victory in the Vietnam War and completed the reunification of the country under communist rule.

And after all these difficult years, the U.S. is now Vietnam's largest trading partner, buying about $7 billion in Vietnamese goods each year. It is also a great tourist destination for many and has found its own identity and peace.

Chapter 12

BACK AT BIÊN HÒA waiting to fly home, our flight was delayed a day. Yes, I should have been out of the army on May 3rd, 1970, but I was still in Nam. On the night of May 3rd, while sleeping on the second floor in one of those half-protected bunkers, we received incoming rockets at 2 o'clock in the morning. I rolled out of the bottom bunk onto the floor and proceeded to get a boot in my face from the guy above as he had jumped down. The waffle pattern it left was on my face for days. It was the final stamp on my tour. One died from this attack, and we should have already been home! Sometimes, the devil wins.

DISENCHANTED
PART 2

Chapter 13

As the plane flew us home, nothing seemed to feel right. It's like looking for the change in your pocket, but it's not there. Sifting through memories sometimes left me with an itch I just couldn't scratch! We arrived at Travis Air Force Base situated in the San Francisco Bay Area, which was the perfect place to be released from the army. As the wheels touched down, there was a big crowd of well-wishers and a marching band. No? Oh yes, just soldiers getting off the plane.

I had extended my tour two months to get out when I landed. I thought doing any army time after Nam would probably have landed me back in the brig or worse. It took three hours of paperwork and a goodbye! What? No parade? No words on the need for help with the VA for PTSD? No thank you for your service, and no fond farewells? So out the door I went in uniform, fully disenchanted.

I was so lucky to have been picked up by Jerry Monet and friends, who had stayed in contact with me and knew my date of release. Jerry had been released a few days before me and you can imagine the picture of "Shell-shocked knuckleheads" driving down the road and celebrating our freedom.

I did some shopping for new clothes, and as we passed Vallejo heading toward Berkeley, with great anger I threw my army shirt right out the car window. Jerry said, "Dude, you are a little nuts," and I said, "Pull the car over."

"What is it man?" Jerry said.

"I just need a minute." I got out of the car, and standing on the side of the road, I stripped every army military item off my body and threw it as far as I could. The cars going by must have thought, What the hell? I wanted to be free of the chains that held me; I held a deep disgust at that moment!

The lack of support, adjusting to stateside environment, and dealing with PTSD had left me caught up in my own tornado with no way out. Confusion was my constant companion as my buddies and I spent the next few days together in California.

The night of May 5th, 1970, we had been out having dinner on a very warm and pleasant evening, walking residential streets of Berkeley. We stopped by a Catholic church with many people holding a single candle, each with sign that read "Stop the War" and "Kent State will not be forgotten."

On May 4, 1970, members of the Ohio National Guard fired into a crowd of Kent State University demonstrators, killing four and wounding nine Kent State students. The impact of the shooting was dramatic. The event triggered a nationwide student strike that forced hundreds of colleges and universities to close.

H. R. Haldeman, a top aide to President Richard Nixon, suggests the shootings had a direct impact on national politics. Haldeman stated that the shootings at Kent State began the slide into Watergate, eventually destroying the Nixon administration. Beyond the direct effects of May 4th, the shootings have certainly come to symbolize the deep political and social divisions that so sharply divided the country during the Vietnam War era.

As we walked by, they asked us if we were military. I said yes and that we had just been released from the army and had done a tour in Vietnam. I will always remember their kindness and concern as they asked us to join them in their vigil as they were holding signs and candles in the dark. In my state of mind, I just could not do it. We were all in unison thinking, we just got back and can't make that call! To this day I regret that choice. Bob Dylan's *The Times They Are A Changing*' was ringing in my ears.

My first car after coming home

Jerry took me around looking for a used car I could drive back to Seattle, and I fell in love with Isabella! Manufactured in Germany from 1951 to 1962, my 1958 Isabella Borgward Station Wagon was going to take me home!

After a farewell to my friends, it was time to drive solo up the coast and head home. Along the way I picked up some hitch-hikers for conversation and got to see this new world through their eyes. As we pulled into Eugene Oregon, a sleepy small town at the time, I stopped for gas. The transmission was acting up, and as I put it in reverse, smashed into the gas pump. All three hitch hikers looked at me with that "Man you need some help" look and gave me that goodbye wave like they were leaving a nuthouse.

Well yes, I did need some help. I paid for the damage and had them check my tranny, and sure enough, it was toast. Oh yeah, I just love those used car salesmen! Just stamp a big "S" on my forehead, for sucker!

How many transmissions for a 1958 Isabella Borgward would I find in Eugene? What are the chances?

But talking with the mechanic I was surprised when he said, "I got a guy that knows a guy that you might want to call." I made the call to the local junk man, who said, "I think I got one in the attic," and sure enough he did! My angels again were guiding me home!

I had a few days staying in the "No Tell Motel" while waiting on the repair and met an American girl. Yes, a real live English-speaking American girl! I had not realized how precious and beautiful it is to be in the presence of a stateside girl until you have been deprived as a young man for fourteen months. She worked as a maid in the hotel and we had time to take some walks and enjoy each other. Welcome home to the U.S. never felt so sweet.

Several days later, Isabella and I were heading home. The purr of the engine and great days of May traveling northbound. As I-5 turned on up around the corner, the Seattle skyline came into view. To be denied your town and then have it in front of you paints your heart with that warm and tender sense that so many songs are written about.

I was coming home to my friends and family, and it was time for a party. Yet I felt like the whole world was spinning faster than I could keep up with. I seemed distracted and confused to all who saw me. My best friend Marty and all those that had written and cared for me were there. Stepmother Mary, Dad and their two sons Mike and Bruce were also there. Of course Dad was having another bad marriage, and Mary tried to have him go to counseling, which didn't go well with him. Why is it always the close-minded that can't see the light? But the best part was they had two sons. who are my dearest friends to this day and helped me through the loss of my own son.

Mary suggested John L. Williams for some counseling, as she saw me troubled, not sleeping, and just not myself. Good 'ole Mary always watching out for me.

The nightmares for that year made it hard to sleep. Rockets going off, guys dying, and the reoccurring one that has me riding in Captain Dickheads Jeep, and he's telling me I had to come back! "Soldier, you just didn't get the job done the first time."

And the survivors guilt always was there for those I lost when I came home, and they went on to Cambodia and didn't come home.

Driving down the street in Isabella on the 4th of July on my way to Mary's house, someone let off one of the two-inch firecrackers in the air above me, and I dove to the floor boards as the car jumped the parking strip and ran into the bushes. Isabella and I were okay, but yes, that was my first Independence Day since Nam.

Chapter 14

THERE ARE MORE SUICIDES BY VETS than the number of those who actually died in Vietnam. It is twenty-two a day, at last count, for all vets. Although flawless counts are impossible to come by—the transient nature of homeless populations presents a major difficulty—the U.S. Department of Housing and Urban Development (HUD) estimates that 39,471 veterans are homeless on any given night.

To keep the people who fought for this country safe when they arrive home, all we need is a mandatory thirty-day decompression. Yes, with counselling and other group activities. Not waiting until they cry out! To save their lives, they need their families, our tax dollars, and an overall sense of goodwill towards them. I just don't get it! You would think one of the largest governmental agencies and the military could figure this out. The generals and military leaders who never had PTSD and who make the choice on this just cannot relate! So they choose to say, "Tough it out, Soldier"

When World War II was over, the troops mostly came home by a two-week boat ride and were able to share their experiences with each other and just talk it out. This was very helpful for many. They also came home as heroes with parades and public approval. Oh yes, and they won the war!

Now we just get on a flight and head home, with little discussion.

So I started sessions with John L. Williams (with my own money) that were once a week. That lasted over a year, dealing with my PTSD and learning rational therapy. Private and group sessions got me to talk about the war. To me, it was so obvious. Hell, I couldn't even buy a hot dog on the street! Yes, that bad. I thought, "Geez, I made it through that damn war and thought coming home, all would be good—and it was worse! So I was the perfect PTSD patient and wanted desperately to get well.

John started teaching me that the mind and your thoughts can be corrected. We have thoughts that are not healthy to us. A neurotic person is one who has bad thoughts but likes to continually think them anyway. So to be aware of my thinking and try to stop the thoughts that were not healthy was my challenge. I read his book and once a week had a session that has made my life so much better. Happy thoughts, healthy thoughts!

But so much of PTSD can be fought simply by an open discussion about the experiences that a person goes through. Whether it's at the V.A. or anyplace trying to help, cognitive therapy, is just expressing how it felt and what it was like through that difficult time. These methods always seem to work the best.

Gary, my buddy who did three tours as a sniper and now works with vets with PTSD, agrees: "It's easier on the guys that are open to talk." It's the quiet guys, he says "that have it the toughest."

I spent my first year of recovery living with my old girlfriend Becky up on Orcas Island in the San Juan Islands one hundred miles north of Seattle. It was the perfect place to heal my heart and soul. This wonderful old cabin overlooked the ferry on Orcas and was equipped with no door handles. Trusting souls back then. Just sliding slats to open the door! Those were the best days of doing little but playing guitar and recuperating from the war. And once a week I would come into Seattle, visit with the folks and friends, stand in line to collect my unemployment, and go to counseling.

The more I got better, the more Becky and I drifted apart. She went off to Colorado, and I went off to try and get a job.

Landing the prestigious job as cleanup crew at Seattle's iconic Space Needle.

There are some similarities between the Space Needle and the Eiffel Tower. The Eiffel Tower was built in 1887 for the World's Fair, and they wanted some great structure to draw people in. At that time so many Parisians hated the structure, and it's the reason that there is an ordinance to this day in Paris that states you cannot build anything higher than six stories!

Eighty-five years later, Seattle did exactly the same thing. The Space Needle was built for the 1962 World's Fair, and the people embraced this new design with open arms, and it has always identified Seattle with its style and grace.

My first day at the Space Needle gave me an indication that I was possibly not long for this employment. As I walked into the service and employee elevator, there was a ten-foot sign imprinted on the concrete that said, "FIRE LANE." I know it was for "No Parking," but it certainly unnerved me.

As I rode the elevator six hundred feet to the top of the mezzanine level, there was a young man and a girl that I thought I recognized. I said, "Don't I know you from Queen Anne High School? She said, "Yes, I'm Yvonne and I was in your English class."

She introduced me to Joe Loutey, and from that day forward all three of us became the best of friends.

Yvonne with her quirky and fun sense of humor, and Joe, my dear Joe, who showed me so much in this life and became the first guidepost of how to find my way. We all get chances in life, but it's what you do with them. I grabbed a hold of this one and hung on tight. The man had a way to discern my youthful impulses and keep me steady. When these types come along, it doesn't happen very often, and when it does, it's only good if you're listening. And I was eager.

Joe, me, and two others worked the night shift cleaning up the restaurant after it closed. We would vacuum and polish and clean the inside of the windows. This massive structure was designed so the floor continuously moved 360 degrees in an hour so that customers constantly saw a new view. All we had to do to clean the windows was stand in one place and wait for the next window to come by. We always completed our mission a little early and had time for a poker game. Those were the days of easy work and good friendships. Nothing so good that man won't come along and screw it up, and of course then management changed the program and hired a service to do the work, and we were then transferred to, yes you got it, Dishwasher.

I was a professional at this kind of work as my very first job, after paper routes, at 16 was dishwashing at Bayview Manor located on the steep slopes of Queen Anne Hill in Seattle. For $1.25 an hour, my first day they had me spinning.

They said, "James, we have a job for you. We need for you to mop out the freezer." In my eagerness I grabbed the mop and bucket of water and proceeded to walk into the giant freezer and start mopping. Of course, the mop stuck to the floor and they were outside having their "new guy giggles." The perfect newbie for the job.

Brother Bill was a waiter at the same facility where they had five hundred tenants, all elderly with care. I'm not sure what's worse, waiting on them or washing five hundred plates, forks, spoons, glasses, and a mountain of pots and pans.

Joe and Yvonne had acquired a selling booth at the Pike Place Market. They would make candles at home and take them to the market to sell .

I started working with them and brainstorming new ideas. That age of innocence and fun ideas made for a terrific combination at that time in our lives. Joe had a bachelor's degree from the University of Washington in sociology, but he was having too much fun to pursue it.

As I got more involved, I started creating candles that had a new and exciting look. We hung sand candles that not only sold at our store, but we merchandised them to many retail outlets throughout the state. My favorite was the invention of the six-pack Rainier Beer candle. It looked just like a beer bottle with the label, except it was made out of wax with a wick at the top. We would put them in six packs and sell them to 7-Eleven's, and they ate them up. Joe and Yvonne said "Lane, we want you to have one-third of the company." I said, "Get me out of the dishwashing job. Hallelujah".

Being the lowest denominator at the space needle, you were the first one to get shit on. If there's a mess, you clean it up. If you have a boss, Laurence, who likes to put folks down, you're high on his list, and a course the girls usually never date the dishwasher.

It was such a pleasure to tell my manager that I was quitting, and he said ,"You can't quit, you're fired." And of course I said %$#^&*).

The day I went back to get my last check, dreading the moment, there was a storm brewing. Winds were howling, and the rain was coming down sideways. Walking over the FIRE LANE sign, I got in alone to ride to the top in the service elevator that was shaking and banging like a bucking bronco.

That moment I realized this was a bad idea. I was three hundred feet in the air, and the elevator stopped. My first thoughts were, "Just don't fall, just don't fall, damn it! Just don't fall."

So it held steady, and the elevator did have a telephone, and it rang. It was Lawrence the manager that had tried to fire me. I think he was enjoying this. He said, "James, I just want you to know that Otis elevator is on strike."

I said "Thanks for the bright news." Thirty minutes went by, and I started seeing the news trucks rolling in with their cameras for the new hot story for the night. You would think that news stations would pay us a percentage for helping them get good ratings. I guess trauma patients just aren't in the mood to negotiate. Bastards!

As I waited, the elevator began banging side to side. I continued to get phone calls from all the pretty waitresses who never gave me the time of day. Now because I was dying or going to be on TV, they all felt so concerned.

Two hours into this madness, they finally were to get an Otis elevator employee there to save me. He scared me more than the damned elevator. He started speaking in this high-pitched nervous tone, saying "Stay away from the door," and don't touch this and don't touch that. Then finally the elevator started moving. Snails run faster!

It took a good hour to travel that last three hundred feet to the kitchen level. Not sure why I went up instead of down, but as the elevator got close to the kitchen level, I couldn't wait any longer, and they had pried the doors open, and I jumped out happy to be out of that damned thing. As I went to stand, I had three cameramen and newspeople all over asking me, "What did it feel like?"

I said, "Let me show you," and tried to put one of them in the elevator.

I said, "Get me a drink and get me my check cause I'm outta here." Of course then I realized I somehow had to get down, but as it turned out, the customer elevators were much more substantial and the wind had died, and before too long I was back on solid ground.

Later in life, when my daughter was 12, I asked her what she wanted for her birthday, and she said, "Dad, let's go to the Space Needle." I said "Oh dear girl, anything but that."

Chapter 15

When I was living in Magnolia in Seattle above a garage for $50 a month! Those were the days. I didn't have to make too many candles to pay the rent. This is when I discovered that my passion was creating and developing new ideas. This was my new life. Find something you're passionate about and do it as work; So rewarding and to me is the American dream.

I would make candles during the day and play and write music on my guitar at night. No health insurance, no car insurance, no cell phone bill, and not even a Comcast bill.

I find it interesting that we now have so many more financial responsibilities than in the 1970's and 80's.

Car insurance became mandatory in Washington State in the 1980's, and that was necessary. New Hampshire and Virginia, however do not require motor vehicle insurance. In New Hampshire, vehicle owners must satisfy a personal responsibility requirement instead of paying monthly premiums and prove they are capable of paying in case of an accident. In Virginia, vehicle owners may pay an uninsured motorist fee instead of insurance.

The federal government has made health insurance mandatory as well. And God forbid we are without our cell phones and TV's. With all these new costs, the federal minimum wage has not kept up!

That $50 a month apartment now costs $500, and yet minimum wage went from $2.65 in 1978 to $7.70 in 2018. My calculations would put the minimum wage at $27 at that rate of increase. That's why we now see so many people working two jobs and still homeless.

> The federal poverty level for 2018 as stated by our government is $13,860. Basically that is the minimum wage at $7.70 per hour with a 40-hour work week.

We had a center aisle booth at the Pike Place Market in Seattle. This was back in the days of the late 70's before it was purchased by the city of Seattle. It was privately owned by Mr. Desimone and had that beautiful simplistic flavor with its creaky boards and continuous hub of characters selling their wares from fish to fandango's. To have a place that all you had to do was invent something that people wanted was so exciting and thrilling for my beginning days. One beautiful day in June, 1974 I had to go and work the booth because our normal person was sick that day

And there she was! The most beautiful brunette came up to the booth with her friend, batted her eyes, and said, "Can you tell me where the bathroom is?"

Oh my God, it took me moments to collect myself and then said, "Yes let me tell you, but before you go, where are you from?"

She said, "I've come back home from living a few years in Santa Cruz, California."

I said, "Oh, lucky me!"

She was thin and tall and had a special quiet way about her, not like so many of the girls I had been with before. I've heard that adage, "It's not what you say but how you make them feel," and oh yes, she sure did make me feel!

She said her name was Laura, and she gave me her phone number, and I couldn't keep my mind off her after she had left.

On our first date I picked her up in my 1961 green Ford pickup truck that she named Sweet Pea. Off we went to see the movie *Zar Doz*. Kind of a goofy movie, but we had fun and began learning about each other.

I was back in the hospital with my second operation on my shoulder, and she was there. I knew then that I had a chance with her.

The VA then paid me $5,000 for my shoulder, and in 1975 Laura and I bought our first house for $13,900 and later on got married.

As time went on, I met her folks and began to understand what it was like to have a kind and loving family that is consistently there for you. Her father became my mentor on how I could break the chain of abuse and difficulties in my new life with Laura. Between her father Howard, Joe, and my best friend Marty, who also came from a strong family, I learned what it was like to travel in their shoes.

One day Marty pulled me aside and said " Listen, this girl, I just want you to know, she is the best, and you better not screw this up."

That advice was well taken, and we went on to live a fulfilling and happy life with two beautiful children, Rachel and Matthew. Yes, I was starting to become happy and not so disenchanted.

Through this life we are given, it is how we listen to friends and mentors that helps us find real happiness. And sometimes it's not what they say but how they make you feel.

Laura and I have had forty-two years of love and happiness. Yes, I found my way back and will always be grateful to all the friends and family that taught me how to make this life a good one. God bless you all!

CPSIA information can be obtained
at www.ICGtesting.com
Printed in the USA
LVHW081506300123
738221LV00013B/836